The Akan House of Mystery

The History and Accomplishments
of the Akan People

I0438144

by
George B. Streetor

Date of Birth 23 June 1948
An Agriculturist and a Homatherapist

Strategic Book Publishing and Rights Co.

Strategic Book Publishing and Rights Co.
12620 FM 1960, Suite A4–507
Houston, TX 77065
www.sbpra.com

ISBN: 978–1-62516–623–4

Typography and page composition by J. K. Eckert & Company

This book is dedicated to the children of Africa.

Contents

Preface

This book has been written to highlight the Akan culture and some of its people, who have made significant accomplishments in society.

The profits from its publication will be used to set up homatherapy centres across Africa. What is homatherapy? It is the ancient practice of healing the atmosphere through the agency of fire in a copper pyramid tuned to the rhythm of sunrise and sunset. As the atmosphere is healed, it heals the contents in the pyramid. Individuals breathing the smoke rising from the pyramid find that their blood is healed by the purified ash, so that no disease can stay in their bodies for a period of three to four months. (See www.homatherapy.org.) It is the only therapy that counteracts radioactivity and cures ailments as varied as insomnia, cancer, kidney stones, gallbladder attacks, and AIDS without the use of chemicals.

The first homatherapy centres supported by the sale of this book will be set up in the Ivory Coast, which shares a border with five other African countries—Guinea, Liberia, Mali, Burkina Faso and Ghana. Developmentally disabled children, as well as children who have AIDS (acquired immune deficiency syndrome), will be treated using homatherapy practices at no cost.

Homatherapy is, unfortunately, not as well known as it should be. The famous pop star, Michael Jackson, died in June 2009 as the result of an overdose of drugs to fight insomnia.

Homatherapy, rather than dangerous pharmaceuticals, would have solved his problem safely. Nelson Mandela, the first post-apartheid president of South Africa, was hospitalised in December 2012 following a gallbladder and kidney-stone surgery. Homatherapy could have solved the problem without resorting to hospitalization or surgery at all.

I am among the first Africans (if not the very first) trained in homatherapy by two renowned practitioners: Dr. Irma Garcias Chaferdet of Venezuela, a solicitor by profession who worked with the United Nations for over twenty years and is now a homatherapy consultant; and Ms. Maria Broom of the United States. I am ready to share this noble science of healing for free to anyone ready to learn and spread it for the benefit of humanity and the preservation of nature.

I believe that the biblical prophet Daniel was speaking of homatherapy when he wrote, "For the morning and evening sacrifices which I am about to tell you, keep it secret for it will take a long time before it will come true." (Daniel 8:26). It was not until recent times that the atmosphere cried out for healing; let us heal the atmosphere and the healed atmosphere will heal us. Buddhists can find the same observation in Sutanipat 568, "agihutto mukho yanya," a Sanskrit phrase explaining that agnihotra (homatherapy) is the basis of all sacrifices. Any agency, governmental or nongovernmental, needing my services in any part of the world (especially Africa) may contact me via email at gbstreetor@gmail.com.

Acknowledgments

I wish to thank the chiefs and people of the Baoule Kingdom for sharing their historical facts with the public.

My sincere thanks go to Fr. Fred Poku Sarkodee of St. Chad Anglican Church, London, United Kingdom; Ms. Comfort Boakye Yeboah of Ontario, Canada; Mr. Stephen Duah of the United Kingdom; Colonel Major Mamadou Comara, aviation advisor to the Minister of Defense, Cote d'Ivoire; Corporal Olivier Kouassi of Gendarmerie, Cote d' Ivoire; M. N'diore Kouame Isidore of SDV Abidjan, Cote d'Ivoire; M. Nzi Gbanan, chief of network office, Cote d'Ivoire; Chris Akuffo Addo, Ghana; M. Nguessan Kouadio Pierre, Cote D'Ivoire; and Mrs. Beryl Enyonam Oppong Adjei, Accra, Ghana, for their support. May the good Lord bless them all.

Introduction

This book is non-fiction, historical, geographical, political, cultural, and spiritual. It is imperative to define the word "Akan" for the benefit of those unfamiliar with it. The Akan people are an important ethnic group of West Africa, comprising over twenty million people. It is the biggest ethnic group in Ghana and Cote d'Ivoire, with a few representative members scattered in other West African countries, such as Togo.

Although the Akan people of Ghana and Cote d'Ivoire share many common customs, cultural practices, and religious beliefs, they are divided into dozens of different tribes. Each tribe speaks its own dialect of the Akan language, Kwa, which is part of the Niger-Congo family. Most Akan-Kwa dialects are easily understood by other Akan.

The proto-Kwa language is believed to have come from East/Central Africa, before its speakers settled in the Sahel. The people who would later become known as the Akan migrated from the Sahel to coastal West Africa. In the twelfth century A.D., the Kingdom of Bonoman was firmly established by the Akan people. Bonoman was a trading state between the Akan and neighbouring people, especially those from Djenne. During various phases of the Bonoman Empire, groups of Akan migrated out of the area to create independent states, sustaining themselves predominantly by gold mining and the trading of farm products.

From the fifteenth to the nineteenth century, the Akan people dominated gold mining and gold trade in the region. From the seventeenth century on, the Akan were among the most powerful groups in West Africa. They fought numerous battles against the European colonists to maintain their autonomy. During the trans-Atlantic slave trade, enslaved Akan, such as the Coromantins of Jamaica and descendants of the Akwamu in St. John's, were responsible for slave rebellions in the New World.

By the early 1900s, all Akan lands in Africa were colonies or protectorates of the French and English. On the 6 March 1957, under the leadership of Kwame Nkrumah (an Akan-Nzima), the Akan in the Gold Coast rejected British rule and joined with formerly British Togoland to form the independent nation of Ghana. Similarly, Felix Houphouet Boigny (an Akan-Baoule) led Cote d'Ivoire to independence on 7 August 1960. A fiercely independent and self-determined people, the Akan cannot stand to be ruled by others.

Some of the modern-day Akan achievers are: Dr. K. A. Busia, the first African student to study at the University College, Oxford, United Kingdom and one-time Prime Minister of Ghana; Kofi Annan, the first black African to head the United Nations for two consecutive terms or mandate; Hon. Paul Yaw Boateng, the first black African Member of Parliament in the United Kingdom; Dr. Mike Agyekum Addo, (a pharmacist and industrialist who supports over two hundred and fifty brilliant but needy students in tertiary institutions in Ghana; and Hon. David Sarpong Boateng, a self-made man who started as a drummer in a dance band and now Ghanas' High Commissioner to Cuba with concurrent accreditation to Jamaica, Trinidad and Tobago, Barbados, Granada, Nicaragua and Panama.

Akan people follow matrilineal rules of ancestry and inheritance. Goods are inherited directly through the mother; children cannot inherit from their fathers because only their mothers know if that man was the biological father or not. Traditionally, children could only inherit from their mother's brother or their sister's son. An Akan belonged to the family of the mother, known as "abusua" (family or dynasty), while he or she is said to be covered by the father's "ntoro" or "sunsum"—soul or spiritual ego. Every Akan family has a family house where deliberations are held. In the Akan tradition, when a king was to be enstooled—the Akan version of a coronation—the queen mother or the elder woman in the family nominated a male royal for the kingship.

Akan political structure is more complex than the paternal inheritance it replaced. One of the reasons for the development of these policies was to prevent the instability created by the higher mortality rate of males. Men tended to die younger due to warfare and dangerous labour.

The Akan also believed that women are more supportive and courageous than men. In the Christian Bible, Mary Magdalene and other women courageously visited the tomb where the body of Jesus was laid after his crucifixion, when the men were in hiding. And in Islamic tradition, the Prophet Mohammed (may peace and blessing be upon him) was able to propagate Islam with the support of two women, Khadija al-Kubra and Aishatu.

Another example of the moral courage of women can be drawn from the history of Ghana itself. In 1900, when the British colonial rulers of Ghana (then the Gold Coast) captured the king of Ashanti, Nana Prempeh I, and exiled him to the Seychelles Islands, Governor Frederick Hodgson also demanded the Golden Stool of Ashanti. The Golden Stool was the embodiment and soul of the people of Ashanti (Asante) and was believed to have been commanded into existence from the sky by the famous Fetish Priest of Asante, Okomfo Anokye, during the reign of Nana Osei Tutu I in the 1600s.

As the kings and queens of Ashanti were deliberating the British demand of the Golden Stool, Nana Yaa Asantewaa, the queen mother of Ejisu, made a powerful statement that inspired the men to defend the stool. She told them, "Now I see that some of you fear to go forward to fight for our king. If it were the brave days of Osei Tutu, Okomfo Anokye, and Opoku Ware, chiefs would not sit down to see their king taken away without a fight. No European could have dared speak to chiefs of Asante in the way the governor spoke to you this morning. Is the bravery of Asante a myth? I cannot believe it. It cannot be. If you men of Asante will not go forward, then we will. I shall call upon my fellow women. We will fight the white men. We will fight till the last of us falls in the battlefields."

With this, Nana Yaa Asantewaa took leadership of the Ashanti uprising of 1900, gaining the support of other members of the Asante nobility. That was the Yaa Asantewaa War, or the War of the Golden Stool, the fourth and last war fought between the Ashanti and the British. After that war, Ashanti was annexed into the Gold Coast Colony under British rule in 1902. Eventually the rebellion was quelled. Yaa Asantewaa was arrested and exiled with fifteen of her advisors to the Seychelles Island, where she died on 17 October 1921.

Three years after her death, King Prempeh and other members of the nobility were allowed to return to Ghana. King Prempeh made sure the remains of Yaa Asantewaa were taken with them, so they would be able to give their courageous queen a fitting burial. Even to this day, Yaa Asantewaa is still a very much-loved person in Ghana.

In conclusion, women are held in high esteem in the Akan society and are accorded respect and dignity as the soul of the family. But as we will see, any woman who did not produce a female child in her lifetime to continue the family line had good reason to feel herself cursed, especially if she was the only surviving female child in that particular family. The lack of a female heir is a serious problem for any family—for without a female heir, the family will die out.

PART I
THE STORY OF THE AKAN

1

The Akan in Ghana

The Akan people in Ghana are made up of a number of different tribes: Ashanti, Ahanta, Akim, Akwamu, Akuapem, Fante, Aowin, Agona, Bono, Assin, Kwahu, Gomoa, Breman, Ahafo, Nzema, and Denkyira. The Akan constitute 49.1% of Ghana's total population. The Akan language, which is the most dominant language in Ghana today, is even spoken by a large percentage of the population who are not Akan.

Akan celebrations cover the rites of passage: childbirth, puberty, marriage, and death. For the majority of the people, these celebrations provide all that is satisfying to their communities and families. Many festivals include a procession of chiefs, tribal leaders and queen mothers, dressed in colourful palanquins, shaded by the traditional umbrellas, and accompanied by drummers and warriors discharging ancient muskets. The entire village participates in the major ceremonies, the most frequent of which are funeral celebrations that typically last several days. Attendance at funerals is normally expected from everyone in the village and expenditure on funerals is a substantial part of a household budget.

The Ashanti is the largest tribe in Ghana. Once renowned for the splendour and wealth of their rulers, they are most famous today for their craftwork, particularly hand-carved stools, pottery, ceramics, jewellery, fertility dolls, and colourful kente cloth. Kente cloth is woven in bright, narrow strips with complex patterns. It is usually made from cotton and is always woven outdoors, exclusively by men. In fact, most crafts are produced by male artisans; only pottery making is primarily a female activity. And even in the case of pottery making, only men are allowed to fashion pots or pipes representing anthropomorphic or zoo-morphic figures.

2

The Akan Tribes in the Ashanti Region

The main Akan tribes in the Ashanti region are: Adansi, Agona, Bekwai, Kumasi, Juaben, (old), Ejisu, Mampong, Offinso, Effiduase, Asante Akyem, Ahafo, Kokofu, Nsuta, Kumawu, and Asokore. All of these groups can be found in the Ashanti region of Ghana except Ahafo (in the Brong Ahafo region for political reasons) and New Juaben, which is in the eastern region where the main story revolves.

Only two non-Ashanti tribes in Ghana supported the Ashanti in their war campaigns against the British and their allies. These two tribes were the Dagomba in the northern part of Ghana and the Nzema in the western region of the country. The Dagomba and the Nzema, together with the Akan, share the term "porcupine warriors." The Ashanti are called Ashanti Kotoko, the Nzema are called Nzema Kotoko, and the Dagomba are called Anwar Kotoko. "Kotoko" doesn't actually mean porcupine—it refers to one who bends low to fight, which is necessary when dodging bullets. Porcupines also bend low when they dislodge their quills at an aggressor. The Ashantis and their two allies are seen as smart, resourceful survivors, a trait that has served them well.

3

The Akan in Cote d'Ivoire

The Akan in Cote d'Ivoire (Ivory Coast), a country that borders Ghana, are made up of a number of smaller tribes: the Agni, Abbey, Attie, Avikam, Aboure, Alladjan, Adjoukrou, Baoule, Abidji, Ehotile, Ebrie, and Nzema (Apollo). Their territories encompass Abidjan, Aboisso, Abengourou, Akoupe, Bouake, Bondoukou, Bongouanou, Sakassou, Tanda, Toumodi, Tiemelekro, Agnibilekro, Sikensi, Tiassale, Ndouci, Agboville, Daoukro, and Dimbokro, as well as a few other locations.

As mentioned earlier, the Akan in Ghana and Cote d'Ivoire share the same cultural identity and greet one another as "abus" (from "abusua," an Akan word meaning family). The word "yaako," an Akan word indicating sympathy for the bereaved, has infiltrated the French language used in Cote d'Ivoire, and is used by both Akan and non-Akan to express sympathy for the victim of a mishap, even of a trivial nature like falling down.

Cote d'Ivoire is made up of over sixty ethnic groups, but the Akan comprises 42.1% of the total population. Within the Akan, the Baoule tribe has fifteen percent of the total population, making it the largest Akan group, followed by the Agni. Most of the Akan tribes migrated to Cote d'Ivoire before the Ashanti's rise to power when Ashanti was still a vassal state to Akwamu and Denkyira. The Baoule tribe (Akan-Ashanti) was led into Cote d'Ivoire by the great Asante warrior-queen Nana Abena Pokua (Abla Poku).

THE ADAKO-BAOULE KINGDOM IN COTE D'IVOIRE

The ancestry of the Adako royal line that rules the Baoule Kingdom of the Akan in Cote d'Ivoire, Ghana, and Togo today is the matriarchal line of its original founder. The Baoule Kingdom was founded in 1720 by Nana Abena Pokua, the female head of the royal family that broke away from the Akan ruling house in Kwaman (Kumasi) after the assassination of Abena Pokua's brother Nana Dako, heir to the throne. The Baoule Kingdom was consolidated by 1730, and from that time until 1760, Nana Abena Pokua reigned as the warrior queen of the Akan in the present day Cote d'Ivoire.

4

The Breaking of the Royal Lineage and its Ties: Oyoko and Adako

Nana Osei Tutu I (King of Akan-Asante) ruled the Asante from 1680 to 1717. He was killed during the civil war between the Asante and the Akyem. At the onset of the struggle, he had underestimated the Akyem because they were few in number, and he went into battle without his usual magical amulets, even leaving some of his body armour back at Kumasi. As he crossed the Pra River in a canoe, he was struck by bullets fired by Akyem snipers and sharpshooters, who were hiding in the dense tree line.

Nana Osei Tutu I died minutes after being shot. His last words were "Anka me nime ya" (if only I knew), an apparent reference to his having underestimated the Akyem. He had gone to war with his grand-nephew, Opoku Ware. After his granduncle's death, Opoku Ware searched desperately for Nana Osei Tutu I's body but unfortunately could not recover it from the Pra River. When he finally returned home, he found that some of the kingmakers from the Adako royal house had nominated his Great-granduncle Nana Dako, heir to the throne and brother of Nana Pokua, as the next reigning monarch. This infuriated Opoku Ware, who had been chosen by the traditional priest Okomfo

Anokye as the successor of his Granduncle Osei Tutu I. He was determined to fulfil his prophetic destiny. In the scuffles that ensued, the Oyoko partisans of Opoku Ware assassinated Nana Dako.

THE DEATH OF NANA DAKO

The assassination of Nana Dako brought about the greatest and perhaps the longest schism that ever erupted in Akan history. Mothers fought against sons, brothers against brothers, sisters against sisters.

Nana Abena Pokua, heir to the throne and leader of the resistance movement against Opoku Ware I, took portions of the royal regalia and paraphernalia and half of the entire royal house to accompany her on a journey that has been called "the trail of tears, liberty and freedom."

THE CIVIL WAR BETWEEN NANA ABENA POKUA AND NANA OPOKU WARE I

In 1719, Nana Abena Pokua mobilised her partisans and moved from Nsuta to Kwaman (present-day Kaase in Ghana). Living among the Nzima/Agni and Sefwi, she adopted their language and even changed her name from Abena Pokua to Abla Poku, thus severing any ties with the Asante. Between 1720 and 1730 Nana Abena Pokua faced many obstacles and confronted life with determination.

The entire army of Opoku Ware I followed the partisans. The capture or arrest of a partisan of Abena Pokua meant automatic execution. Many of the Adako royals were killed together with their Akuona supporters. When Nana Abena Pokua moved about the countryside, war and destruction followed. Civil war had engulfed the Asante Kingdom.

From 1717 to 1720, the Asante Kingdom was in tumult, civil strife raged, and the Adako-Oyoko royal household was divided. For three years, the family was unable to select a successor to the throne. For members of both royal houses, the death of Nana Dako and the subsequent civil war that ensued was the most painful event in the history of the family. For Nana Opoku Ware I, the division of his family and the breakaway of a major part of the family were devastating; he wished that Nana Dako was alive and Nana Abena Pokua had not rebelled.

The Oyokos, the nephews of the Adakos headed by Opoku Ware, kept control of the Oyoko clan and the Golden Stool of Asante while Nana Abena Pokua, the queen mother, remained in exile in Kaase,

Kumasi (formally Kwaman) with her partisans, numbering about three-and-a-half million—about half the population of Asante. Nana Opoku Ware 1 was enstooled as Asantehene (king) in 1720 and his mother Nana Nyarko Kusi Amoa, the niece of Nana Abena Pokua, was also enstooled as the queen mother of Asante. However, as king he needed to unify his new nation and show national solidarity and continuity.

The task of Nana Abena Pokua, on the other hand, was preserving the most sacred of family dreams—heritage. She needed to save the Adako royal family and the only way possible was to go away to create a new nation in an unknown land. The decision by Nana Abena Pokua's own family to resist and bring about schism was not an easy one. The trail she needed to follow now was full of uncertainties, tears, losses, death, depravation, and sacrifices for all who embarked on that journey.

SACRIFICE AND MIRACLE AT THE RIVER COMOE

Upon reaching the Comoe River in what is now Cote d'Ivoire, Nana Abena Pokua found the river flooded and impossible to cross. It would take several weeks to make a boat, and they did not have that kind of time. Knowing that the partisans of Opoku Ware I was on their trail, they had no time to waste. The Tano deity, Akora, was consulted, and they were advised that if they wanted to be saved from the armies of Opoku Ware I, they needed to sacrifice the child of Nana Abena Pokua to the gods and the Comoe River. As the philosophical thinking of Akan was imbued with religious beliefs based on fetishism, juju or voodoo, Abla Pokua felt she had no choice but to sacrifice her child to save the multitude of people who had followed her.

Ceremonies were performed, prayers said, and in accordance with customs and tradition, Nana Pokua offered her son to be sacrificed. After the ceremony, the water in the river started moving and a herd of hippos appeared in the river. The hippos lined up to form a bridge, and the people crossed the river on the animals' backs to reach safety and freedom.

The miracle that took place that day also gave the name to the new kingdom that they founded afterward. In the Twi or Akan dialect, the phrase "ba no awu" means "the child of Nana is dead." It later became Baoule, the name of the new nation founded by Nana Abena Pokua in the present-day Cote' D'Ivoire.

Immediately after the followers of Nana Abena Pokua reached the opposite side of the river, the armies of Opoku Ware I arrived at the river. Some of the brave soldiers attempted to cross, but the hippos moved under the water and all those who attempted to mount on their backs drowned in the Comoe River.

Another legend resulted from this miraculous event. Before Nana Abena Pokua reached the midpoint of the river, a giant rose out of the water and handed her a golden stool, the throne on which Nana Abena Pokua would sit to build the Baoule kingdom. (Interestingly, the Asantehene or king of Asante also occupies a supreme office symbolized by the "sika dwa kofi" or Golden Stool, which is held to embody the "sunsum" or national soul of the Asante people in Ghana.) The adoption of this significant Asante symbol by the new kingdom of Baoule would seem to indicate a passing of the legitimate sceptre from one dynasty to the other, but at the same time the fundamental oneness of the Akan culture.

After the passage, the rear vanguard of Nana Abena Pokua's army decided to settle at the edge of the river. They kept the golden umbrella and the sword of Nana Osei Tutu I as a token of their sacrifice and as a symbol of the unity of the Akan in Cote d'Ivoire.

Whatever the interpretation of the events by the Comoe River on that fateful day, the Akan in Cote' d'Ivoire know beyond any reasonable doubt that God Almighty was with their ancestors and assisted them in crossing the Comoe River. The place where the miraculous bridge of liberty appeared is visible to this day. The Akan go to this site every year to pour libation in honour of the ancestors and in remembrance of their faith in God and their tenacity of purpose that resulted in the creation of a new nation.

Having succeeded in crossing, Nana Abena Pokua's party came to the region known today as Bouake. There she and her followers fought the Senoufou in the north, the Guru in the west, and the Denkyiras, who were earlier defeated by Osei Tutu I at the battle of Feyiase. By 1730, Nana Abena Pokua had subdued all her enemies and had established a powerful empire with a capital at Warebo, based on the constitutional monarchy model introduced by King Osei Tutu. She became the first queen mother of the kingdom and reigned for thirty years. They say, "The camel can go a long way without water, but who dares to be a camel?" Nana Abena Pokua sacrificed her son to build a new kingdom.

5

Nana Houphouet Boigny, the First President of Cote d'Ivoire

All the Akan thrones in Cote d'Ivoire, including that of the Denky-iras at Setikran, owe allegiance to the Akan throne established by Nana Abena Pokua, the first Asante queen and founder of the kingdom of Baoule. Nana Abena Pokua's statue stands in the centre of Abidjan, the capital of Cote d'Ivoire, in memory of her bravery and selflessness. Her male descendant, Nana Baffour Gyanko Fofie I, still lives in the palace she established in Sakassou, and he is honoured by the Baoule and the Akan as their nominal head and king.

But he is not the political leader of Cote d'Ivoire. Nana Houphouet Boigny, having been enstooled in 1958 as the supreme ruler of the Ada-kon Dynasty and of all Akan, was able to accomplish his mission by securing independence for the Ivorian people in August 1960. Thus he is the first President of Cote d'Ivoire—and this is how that came to be.

Nana Baffour Gyanko Fofie I, Nana Abena Pokua's descendant and the current supreme head of the Adako Imperial Dynasty, was enthroned at the age of fifteen, having been traditionally prepared to take over after Nana Kouakou Anougble II. But just before Nana Anougble went to Nana Baffour's village, Nana Houphouet asked Nana Anougble to bless him and empower him to seize the entire country from the French colonizers, and that was what happened. Upon Nana

Anougble II's death in 1958, the powers of the throne were passed on to Nana Houphouet as the next supreme ruler of the Adakon Dynasty, although Nana Guei was also enstooled and he remained a regent until his death in 1978.

Houphouet Boigny, as the first president of Cote' d'Ivoire, brought unity, peace, and development to the Ivorian people. There were no ethnic divisions or tribal sentiments. Cote d'Ivoire was identified as a "jewel of West Africa" by its neighbouring African countries, a model of economic prosperity and political stability. When in 1990 Nana Houephouet realised that his intellectual prowess was diminishing, he appointed a non-Akan, a native of Kong from the northern part of Cote d'Ivoire, to be his prime minister. An economic guru and a man of great intellectual acumen, his name was Dr. Allassane Dramane Ouattara. At that time Dr. Ouattara was the head of the Central Bank of West Africa (BCEAO—Banque centrale des États de l'Afrique de l'Ouest).

Nana Houphouet Boigny died in 1993 after thirty-three years as president, and was succeeded by Henry Konan Bedie, an Akan Baoule, who shared the same aspirations as his predecessor, having been with him as his speaker of parliament. Konan Bedie's presidency was short-lived due to an intrusion by the military, led by General Robert Guei. The military had no mandate to rule a country and this brought a lot of divisiveness to the country. Nevertheless, His Excellency Konan Bedie's political maturity is evident for all to see, considering the chaos that characterised the 2010 elections, which nearly brought the country to its knees. H. E. Konan Bedie asked his supporters to rally behind someone who could bring about peace, stability, and development without ethnic divisions—namely, H. E. Dr. Allassane D. Ouattara, the one-time prime minister, who shared the same aspirations as his mentor, Felix Houphouet Boigny.

6

Akan Names

The Akan attach great importance to the day of the week on which their children are born, since these days determine the nature of their platonic souls. In the Akan tradition, the day of a child's birth determined the child's first name, after which the family or father's name was added. It was the same with other minority Akan tribes in Cote d'Ivoire, except for the Baoule. There the name of the day of birth was determined by the time zone and whether the birth occurred before or after noon.

There are other superstitions regarding birth. For example, the first child in a family is assumed not to be overly clever, while the third is considered precocious and incorrigible. The ninth brings happiness and the tenth spells misfortune. The first president of Ghana, Kwame Nkrumah, wrote, "I can legitimately claim to be following the established order, since I was born on a Saturday and named Kwame. However, it is definitely discouraging to be the first and only child of my mother; hence, according to tradition, less brilliant than the average one."

ADULTERATION OF NAMES

Migration into Cote d'Ivoire, intermarriage with other ethnic groups, and colonization by the French caused most Akan names to change dramatically. For example, a female may be called Miss Yao Kouassi or Miss Yao—which would literally mean she took the name of her father's day of birth as her father's surname. Similarly, one might hear a man called Kouassi Koffi, which is not possible because that would mean he was born on two different days of the week and had no father at all.

Complicating matters further, most of the names had been pronounced in French and subsequently misspelled, leading to tremendous variation in spelling and ultimately meaning.

Not all Akan names follow typical naming patterns. In the Akan tradition, a woman who had experienced a string of miscarriages or early infant deaths would not give her next baby a proper name. For example, the first president of Cote d'Ivoire, a Baoule, was given the name Houphouet (meaning garbage) when he was born. His second name, Boigny, meant a male sheep with well-matured horns. Felix was just a colonial name. Hence, Felix Houphouet Boigny.

ISSUES WITH AKAN WOMEN AND NAMES

In view of the matrilineal inheritance of the Akan people, a woman who became pregnant as a result of a relationship with a non-Akan male would give an Akan name to the child apart from whatever name the father had given, especially when there was no marriage. Another example is the first president of Ghana, who was named Francis Nwiah by his Liberian father, but was later given an Akan name, Kwame Nkrumah, by the family.

7

New Juaben

The state of New Juaben in the eastern region of Ghana is presently comprised of eight distinct communities, namely, Suhyien on the northern border; Akim Abuakwa, Jumapo, Oyoko, Asokore, and Effiduase to the south; and Ada on the border with Yilo Krobo. To the west, Akwadum boasts Koforidua as its capital, on the border with Akuapem.

New Juaben was founded in 1875 as the result of two civil wars—in 1832 and 1875—between Kumasi and Juaben, two of the most prosperous states in the Asante union. Juaben Asante had been an established state for nearly two centuries prior to the formation of the Asante union. Under skillful leadership from Nana Amponben Afra (1530–1550) to the first two kings, Adarkwa Yiadom (1670–1715) and Osei Hwedie (1715–1730), Juaben developed into one of the largest pre-union Asante states through the conquest and subsequent incorporation of less powerful states in the area. One of the last states to fall was the Assin Dynasty under King Ntiamoah Amankuo (his grandson being the present Amakomhene-Kumasi, Abosohene sub-chiefs of Old/New Juaben).

Juaben was one of the five established states that joined in a coalition to form the Asante union. The people of Juaben, who were renowned for their courage and military prowess, played a crucial role in the war between Ashanti and Denkyira that led to the victory and subsequent establishment of the Ashanti nation with Kumasi as its capital. Juaben's King Adarkwa Yiadom triggered the war by rejecting the outrageous demands of Ntim Gyakari, the king of Denkyira. The Juaben army, under the command of Adarkwa Yiadom, captured and killed Ntim Gyakari.

In recognition of the important and decisive roles played by the kings of Kumasi and Juaben, the former was appointed the head of the Asante union, the Asantehene, and the latter was appointed the Oyoko-hene of Asante. The union of Asante comprised five states, and Kumasi had to confer with Juaben in all decisions, and they worked closely to promote the union. The smooth and spirited cooperation between the two brotherly states of Juaben and Kumasi from the second half of the eighteenth century to the third part of the nineteenth century helped the union grow into an empire, encompassing an area even larger than the modern state of Ghana. Unfortunately, not all good things last.

8

Invasion and First Migration

In August 1826, the Ashanti army suffered its first defeat at the hands of the British and their allies at Akatamanso near Dodowa. In the confusion, the Akwamus captured the Golden Stool. Nana Kwasi Boateng, the king of Juaben, swore to recapture it and he did precisely that. But instead of praising and rewarding him for his bravery, the Asantehene, Osei Yaw Akoto, accused him of stealing some gold dust that was kept with the Golden Stool. The Juabenhene felt so offended that he refused to go to Kumasi. Juaben-Kumasi relations deteriorated, war broke out and Kumasi invaded Juaben in 1832.

The uprising was a revolt against Asante laws, customs, traditions, and particularly against the pact of Okomfo Anokye, the shrewd politician-priest, who had decreed that under no circumstance should either Kumasi or Juaben take up arms against the other. Nana Kwasi Boateng defended his state with courage, but in the end he was forced to emigrate with his subjects to Akyem Abuakwa.

Osei Yaw Akoto died in 1834 and was succeeded by Nana Kwaku Dua I. In 1838 the new Asantehene sent emissaries to Akyem Abuakwa to persuade the Juabens to return to Ashanti with the assurance that Nana Kwasi Boateng would be restored to his former status in Juaben and in the confederacy. Nana Boateng reluctantly yielded to the call of the Asantehene and left Kyebi in late 1839 with members of the royal family, including his mother, Queen Ama Juaben Serwah.

18

Nana Boateng suddenly became ill and died at Saaman, near Osino. His only surviving brother, Kofi Boateng, inherited the Stool as Juabenhene and resumed the journey back to Ashanti. Unfortunately, he soon died at Obo Kwahu. The two surviving members of the royal household, Queen Ama Serwah (mother of the late kings) and her daughter Afrakoma, led their people back to Juaben in 1841. The queen occupied the Juaben Stool for four-and-a-half years, during which she tried hard to reconstruct the state of Juaben. When she died in 1846, her daughter Afrakoma succeeded her. Upon the death of Afrakoma, her daughter Akua Saponmaa became the Omanhene of the Juaben state.

9

The Great Migration Under King Asafo Agyei

Queen Ohemaa Saponmaa married her cousin Nana Agyei Twum, son of Kwasi Boateng. The couple had two daughters, Akosua Afrakoma and Akua Boatemaa. Oral tradition has it that when Ohemaa Saponmaa died, Agyei Twum was appointed as caretaker of the Stool until his royal children came of age. However, ambition got the better part of Agyei Twum and he continued to call himself Juabenhene (king of Juaben) under the stool name of Asafo Agyei.

His conduct outraged the rulers of the other Oyoko clan states of the Asante confederacy—Kokofu, Bekwai, Nsuta and Kumasi—as Asafo Agyei was not of Juaben royal blood or a member of the Oyoko clan. The beginning of his reign was marked by acrimony and dissension. As it turned out, however, Asafo Agyei proved to be a great king and soon succeeded in rebuilding and reuniting the state, re-establishing peaceful and friendly relationships with Kumasi and neighbouring Asante states such as Effiduase and Asokore, and winning back the allegiance and support of such vassal states as Krakye and Bassa. He was also able to establish very strong trade links between Juaben and Salaga, the important terminus of the lucrative caravan trade between Hausaland and Ghana.

By the early 1870s, Juaben had become one of the most powerful and prosperous states in the Asante Union. By 1875, Nana Kofi Kari-kari (then Asantehene) attacked Juaben under the pretext of recrimination for King Asafo Agyei's insubordinate behavior. As a result of this attack, the subjects of Effiduase, Asokore, and Oyoko all migrated once again to Akyem Abuakwa in the east. King Asafo Agyei and his compatriots, Yaw Omane, chief of Effiduase, and Anka Akyemfuor, chief of Asokore, travelled subsequently to Cape Coast to petition the British government for ammunition to continue the war against Asante, but they were declined. The bulk of the migrants became squatters on the lands around the site of modern Koforidua.

In March 1877, the government began negotiations with the king of Akyem Abuakwa, Nana Ampao, for land to resettle the Juaben people in the vicinity of Kukurantumi. However, King Asafo Agyei resisted the government's efforts to resettle his people in the Kukurantumi forest. He was arrested and detained in Elmina Castle on August 4, 1877 and exiled to Lagos, Nigeria, a few months later, together with Yaw Omane and Anka, for persistently plotting to renew the war with Asante. In February 1878 the Juaben chiefs informed Governor Freeling of their willingness to settle at once on the land the government had offered them. Within a few weeks the Juaben chiefs arrived at the present site of Koforidua to lay the foundation of the modern state of New Juaben.

Initially, after the Juaben emigrants occupied the Kukurantumi forestland the government had offered them, the people were afraid to stay. Their new homeland was a thick forest in which hunters stalked their game by night, and one could hear the roaring voices of wild animals in the darkness. But being determined, the elders decided to pitch their camps just under the Obuo Tabri Mountain, a sacred mountain that joins the Afajato Mountain through the Kwahu Scarp. That is the reason why the New Juaben palace was built in the shadow of the Obuo Tabri Mountain, and most of the chiefs live on Srodae Street even today ("srodae" being an Akan word meaning "if you are afraid, sleep"). Most of the Juaben people were too frightened to go out after six o'clock in the evening.

But others did not feel that way at all. The town, Koforidua, derived its name from the son of the King of Akim Abuakwa, Kwadjo (Koo) Ofori. He was a regular hunter in the forest. He used to clean his game under a big tree with a river flowing under it, and this came to be used as a description of the whole area—Koo Ofori Dua—Koo Ofori's Tree. Eventually, the name became Koo fori dua and later Koforidua.

Rather than relying on hunting in the forests, the hard-working Juaben people began farming the excellent soil, and within a very short time Koforidua and its environs were leading in the production of exportable crops such as cola nuts and cocoa, as well as maize, plantain, cocoyam, citrus, tomatoes, onions, and mushrooms for local consumption. Later the colonial administration would link up a railway line from Accra through Koforidua to Kumasi, which would help in the transportation of goods and passenger services. That would become an important road and rail junction.

The new towns built by the Juaben were conceived as "extensions" of the migrants' hometowns in Ashanti. Hence those from Effiduase, Asokore, and Oyoko named their new towns after their old ones in Ashanti. The others from Juaben-Ashanti settled in Koforidua, Ada, Akwadum, Jumapo, and Suhyien. Some of the migrants founded their own communities in the heartland of Akyem Abuakwa. Settlements founded here included Ngeresi, Kankan (Sekyere), Abekoase, and Akadewaso. Until the early twentieth century, all these groups owed allegiance to the New Juaben state. Other migrants who settled as individuals in Akyem communities owed allegiance to Kyebi. This category of Juabens could be found in Asuom, Kyebi, Osino, Osiem, Tafo, Kukurantumi, Apedwa, Osenase, Nkronso, and Kwaben.

In May 1879, some fifteen months after the foundation of the New Juaben state was laid, Yaw Omane and Anka were repatriated from Lagos, Nigeria. Early in October of the same year, the new governor of the Gold Coast colony, Herbert Taylor Ussher, had King Asafo Agyei repatriated to Accra and released to join his people at Koforidua. But Asafo Agyei proved unrelenting in his animosity towards Asante and was exiled to Lagos for the second time on November 8, 1880, mere weeks after the death of Queen Afrakoma in Accra on October 26, 1880. Between November 3, 1880 and August 1885, four petitions for the repatriation of Asafo Agyei were turned down by the Colonial Governor W. B. Griffith. However, he paid for the passages of the king's son Asafo Boateng and daughter Boatemaa to visit their father in Lagos for nineteen days. About eight months after their return, news was received of the death and burial of King Asafo Agyei in Lagos.

Until 1898 a triumvirate comprised of Chief Akyeampong Kwasi, Chief Okyere, and Chief Asafo Boateng managed the state affairs of New Juaben on behalf of Princess Boatemaa. In October 1901, Boatemaa left for Juaben Ashanti. In her absence, Chief Okyere and the princess's brother, Asafo Boateng, acted as caretakers. In June 1907, the chiefs of New Juaben elected Asafo Boateng as their head chief and petitioned the government for his formal recognition as Omanhene (king) of New Juaben. As the government recognised the need to rally the New Juaben settlements around a central stool at Koforidua, it approved the consecration of a paramount stool for the New Juaben state and supported the establishment of Asafo Boateng, son of the late King Asafo Agyei, as the first Omanhene of New Juaben.

With the issue of kingship settled (and with the active support and cooperation of Princess Boatemaa), it became necessary to assign responsibilities to the stool bearers—those who would serve as the king's court or cabinet. The Effiduasehene became the Nifahene (right-wing commander), the Asokorehene became the Benkumhene (left-wing commander), while the stool occupants from Juaben-Ashanti retained their respective titles. Chiefs were appointed for Oyoko, Akwadum, Suhyien, Jumapo, and Ada. In the early 1940s the Oyoko-hene was made the Adontenhene (commander of the vanguard). The ten divisions of the present New Juaben state are based on these early positions.

Nana Asafo Boateng died in 1921 and was succeeded by Nana Kwaku Boateng I, a member of the royal family of Juaben-Ashanti and son of Queen Ama Serwaa. It was during his reign that the present palace at Koforidua was built and a number of mission schools established in the state. When he died in 1930, he was succeeded by his cousin, Osei Hwedie. Nana Osei Hwedie's successor was his own brother, Adarkwa Yiadom, who occupied the stool on two occasions. In the interval was Nana Yaw Sarpong, who was succeeded by Nana Adarkwa Yiadom. After him was Nana Akrasi, who was succeeded by Nana Kwaku Boateng II, ruling from 1962 to 1990. His reign of twenty-eight years saw the modernisation of the New Juaben state.

Kwaku Boateng II promoted social and economic activities, playing a leading part in attracting the Workers' Brigade to Koforidua. He also promoted the establishment of a number of secondary and preparatory schools, and played an important role in the transfer of the regional

House of Chiefs from Dodowa to Koforidua. He was an outspoken advocate of improved delivery of utilities such as water, telephone service, and electricity within the traditional area.

Daasebre Kwaku Boateng II also made it his mission to foster cordial and effective links with old Juaben, Kumasi, and the other states of Ashanti. To further closer and more cordial relationships between Ashanti and the New Juaben state, Kwaku Boateng II invited the Asantehene, Otumfuo Opoku Ware II, to Koforidua in 1985 as part of the Golden Jubilee celebration of the restoration of the Ashanti confederacy. That visit had a tremendous impact on the entire population of the New Juaben state. In 1990, Daasebre Kwaku Boateng II died. He was succeeded by Daasebre Oti Boateng.

Daasebre Oti Boateng, Omanhene of New Juaben, was a member of the International Civil Service Commission (ICSC) of the United Nations (Commissioner of the UN from 2003–2007). He holds a bachelor of science in economics from the University of Ghana, master of science in statistics from the London School of Economics and a Ph.D. in statistics from the University of Liverpool, United Kingdom. He was installed in 1992 under the stool name Daasebre. Dr Oti Boateng is a member of the Yiadom-Hwedie royal family of Juaben, Ashanti, and New Juaben, as well as son of the late queen mother of Juaben and blood brother of his predecessor, Nana Kwaku Boateng II. He had a distinguished service career in both government and academia, and now serves as a member of the U.N. International Civil Service Commission (ICSC). Daasebre Oti Boateng is a good academician who has served Ghana's government to the best of his ability, but whether history will see him as a good traditional ruler is another matter. Even after reigning for so many years, he is losing popularity as Omanhene, and is now being threatened by Barima Topen Siribuo with destoolment charges—such as allegedly not sleeping in the palace since he was enstooled as Omanhene twenty-two years ago.

Barima Topen Siribuo is the nephew of Nana Kwaku Boateng II, the former Omanhene. Barima Topen Siribuo was a potential successor to the throne after the death of his uncle, but as he was being groomed for this position, Daasebre Oti Boateng was dramatically sworn in–an affront from which the former king's nephew has apparently never recovered. I wish to use this book to appeal to Barima Topen Siribuo to exercise restraint and avoid friction, animosity, and enmity. Surely it is very painful to be sidelined as a royal, but chieftaincy disputes are ene-mies of progress and must be avoided, for if nature will be fair, the old man will go to his village soon and the kingmakers may not consider Barima Topen Siribuo for the position if the relationship between the present and future kings has been too contentious.

Royals who aspire to become chiefs when a stool is vacant should think of what they can do for the people. They should not just wish to be chiefs because they want to be called Nana and wear *batakari* and sandals. Our chiefs should do their best to address the real needs of their people, including improving the lives of women in Africa who suffer too much as a result of poverty, lack of education, lack of birth control, and lack of legal protection from molestation. The new Oman-hene should look at these and other human-rights issues and try to bring Africa into step with the rest of the modern world.

PART II
THE DESCENDANTS OF YAA AKYAA

10

Consulting a Deity

In the early part of the 1900s, at Koforidua in the eastern region of Ghana (then the Gold Coast), there lived a young woman named Yaa Akyaa. Yaa, as she was affectionately addressed by friends and family members alike, had delivered her first child, a son, at the age of sixteen and named him Kwame Boateng. Most Akan women expected to have a child every two years, but after ten long years of trying, there was no sign of a second pregnancy. Yaa tried all kinds of herbal medicines, to no avail. During that time, Western medicine was rare, and would have been reserved for life-and-death matters, not something as minor as infertility. Yet Yaa needed a baby girl to continue the family lineage of succession, as the Akan custom demanded.

Yaa and her cousin Afia Brago were the only young females in that particular family. Afia Brago was about ten years younger than Yaa. Afia Brago was a very beautiful and shapely girl, one of the loveliest girls among her peers at that time. When Afia Brago turned sixteen, the Omanhene (king) of the New Juaben traditional area, Nana Asafo Boateng, sought her hand in marriage.

Kings in those days had many wives who lived in various family houses, and visited the king on a weekly rotation. Just about six months after the marriage was contracted, Afia Brago decided to go to market to purchase some food to prepare dinner for the king. She took her basket from where she kept it under a tree in the family house and put it on her head to go to the market. On her way to the market, a small snake emerged from the basket and bit Afia on the neck. She started screaming for help, but before people could ascertain what was happening to the young wife, she was dead.

The king, Nana Asafo Boateng, was informed and in order to uphold the Akan custom, he decided to appoint a linguist from that family to honour his beloved young wife. Ten-year-old Kwame Boateng, the only male child of Yaa Akyaa, had to be appointed to that position as the only surviving close relative to the king's dead wife. Kwame Boateng therefore swore an oath of allegiance to the Omanhene, making Akan history as the youngest linguist.

The death of Afia Brago compounded the already precarious situation of Yaa Akyaa as the only surviving female in that family; she had to produce a female child to continue the line of succession. Upon advice from the family members, she decided to consult a witch doctor at a fetish shrine at Adweso, near Koforidua, two kilometres away. After spiritual consultations and rituals conducted by the witch doctor at the shrine, she was given some herbs in which to bathe for a number of days.

In a matter of three months, Yaa was pregnant. She went back to the shrine to inform the witch doctor, who followed up with additional instructions—for example, she was not supposed to bathe with soap after eight o'clock at night during her entire pregnancy. She made sure she never broke any of the rules the doctor gave her. And in nine months' time, on a Thursday night, Yaa delivered a tiny, jet-black, beautiful baby girl, very hairy from the head to the waist. Yaa took the baby to the shrine and was given a concoction to reduce the amount of body hair. She assured all the astonished friends and family members who visited her that the hair would thin out, but they could only reply, "When?" (The Akan word for "when" is "daben.") Since the baby was born on Thursday, the child was to be called Yaa according to the Akan naming tradition, but in view of the incessant question of "Yaa, daben?" no surname was added to the Yaa, but rather she was just called Yaa Daben.

Yaa Daben grew up steadily, and even though the witch doctor's concoction had reduced some of the hair on her body, the hair on her head was still unusually thick and luxuriant. At the age of two years, she had grown extremely beautiful, jet black in complexion with piercing eyes and a sturdy little form. However, she was slow in learning to walk, which caused her family some concern. Madame Yaa Akyaa consulted the witch doctor again to make sure she was not bewitched by any wizard or witchcraft, but was told there was nothing to worry about.

And sure enough, just as Yaa Daben started walking, Maame Yaa Akyaa became pregnant again. She delivered another baby girl on a Wednesday and named her Akua Badu. According to the Akan tradition, the surname or family name Badu was normally given to a tenth-born child, but in that particular case, the baby was named after the mother of Maame Yaa Akyaa, whose name was Badu. The naming ceremony took place one week after birth as custom demanded, and everyone was thrilled that Yaa Akyaa and the family had been blessed with another baby girl to sustain her lineage should she die. The newborn baby resembled Yaa Daben, but was less hairy in comparison. Like her sister, she was also jet black in complexion with silky curly hair on her head.

The Akan tribe normally made sure that for the first three months after a woman had given birth to a newborn baby, a sumptuous meal was prepared for her by noon at the latest. The meal prepared typically include palm-nut soup with healing herbs, to make sure the woman became healthy and at the same time had enough breast milk to feed the newborn baby. And it was no different in Maame Yaa's case. Fufu (a mixture of plantain and cassava, cocoyam, and cassava or yam) was pounded in mortars and eaten with soup prepared from smoked fish. By eleven o'clock every morning, one could hear the sound of mortars and pestles in that house, and the food prepared in such a quantity that visitors could be served without any danger of shortage.

11

The Wedding of Yaa Daben

Yaa Daben did not go to school, even though the colonial masters had introduced schools to the Gold Coast. But the schools reinforced Christianity, which many Akan still believed to be the white man's way of worship and slow in action, as opposed to the traditional mode of worshipping nature gods and idols, which to the Akan was superior and quicker in action.

At the ripe age of fifteen, Yaa Daben was a black beauty, her thick curly hair cascading down below her waist. She had well-shaped buttocks with legs to match, and sizeable apple-shaped breasts with pointed nipples showing through her dress. Both her appearance and her cute personality caused every man, whether young or old, to want her as a wife. Men of all ages tried to win her hand in marriage but all to no avail; the family wanted to make sure she got the right man who could cater to her needs.

Finally a suitor who was a certificated teacher presented himself. Teaching was considered a noble profession and, at least at the end of every month, there was the likelihood of a steady and sustainable income. The lucky man was Mr Asianoa, a respected man in society and in the Anglican church. A date for the marriage was set and after paying the knocking fee (kokooko) and performing the customary marriage rites to the family, arrangements were made to have the wedding take place in the Anglican church. In those days, church weddings were not as common as traditional Akan ones, in which the two families met on the day of the marriage with drinks from the man to the family of the wife-to-be or bride. Libations were then poured to the ancestors of both the husband-to-be and the wife-to-be to bless the marriage. The elders in both families advised the couple, after which more drinks were served to the members of the family and their invited guests.

In the case of Mr. Asianoa and Yaa Daben, both the traditional and church weddings were to take place, and it was a much-anticipated time of joy for both sides due to the beauty of the bride and the popularity of the groom. The pomp and pageantry started on a Saturday, when the traditional rites were performed and continued on Sunday in the church where the Anglican wedding took place. As there were fewer motor vehicles in those days, the couple had to walk the kilometre from the church to their house after the wedding with a big umbrella covering them from the blazing sun. The couple was cheered by onlookers who had come from all nooks and crannies to have a glimpse at the newly-weds.

In the evening, a big party was organised in the family house of the bride with relatives from both sides, invited and uninvited guests, young and old, served rice and chicken stew. In those days, eating rice was not so common and especially with chicken in gravy. Eating chicken and rice only occurred during festivities like Christmas, New Year's Day, and the like. Even during those festivities, the children ate only the head, legs and neck of the chicken, with the rest given to the elderly and the respected in the family.

At that particular party, everyone was served their fill of soft drinks and hard liquor apart from the normal food. In those days there was no Coca Cola or Fanta, but they did have other soft drinks, as well as the local drink tapped from the palm tree. The guests enjoyed listening to highlife music played on a gramophone machine (phonograph). There were also local drummers playing traditional music to satisfy the old folks. The older people also enjoyed dancing to the traditional music; every dance had a language of movements with meanings that had been developed through centuries. It was a great joy for the family of Yaa Daben, especially her mother, and it delighted the people in Koforidua, who had never witnessed such an event in their whole lives.

Sadly, though, seven days after the marriage ceremony, Maame Yaa Akyaa, the mother of Yaa Daben, died in her sleep after complaining of a headache the previous night. She had accomplished her mission and established a family line of succession by producing two female children to continue the lineage as Akan custom demanded, but it was a big blow to the family and the newly married couple. After the burial and the necessary rituals settled as the dust settles after a windy rain, Yaa Daben succeeded her mother as the family matriarch as demanded by the Akan customs.

12

The Linguist

Kwame Boateng, the elder brother of Yaa Daben, never attended school, but was very intelligent and witty. At the ripe age of twenty-five years, he had become one of the best linguists in the New Juaben palace. In the Akan tradition, a linguist or "okyeame" is part spokesperson, part lawyer, and part intermediary. Because commoners do not normally address the king directly, they approach the okyeame with their problems, and the okyeame advocates for them before the king.

A slender, fair-coloured, tall young man, Okyeame Kwame Boateng had mastered the craft of linguistics and was well versed in tradition to present cases to the king. He had the ability to craft words that could best be understood by the king in their presentation. He could listen to litigants' stories and advise them how their cases should be presented so they might win. And he himself could decide on the fate of a case that was to be presented to the king. That made him so popular that people flocked to present cases to him to forward to the king.

Even though Kwame Boateng was well liked and highly respected, he was certainly not the only linguist among the Juaben. Every sub-chief had his own linguist, but when a case was to be deliberated in the palace, only the palace linguists presented them. People could therefore contact anyone of the linguists in their various homes about their problems or presentation of cases to the king to be settled. Minor cases that did not affect the state or kingdom could be settled by the sub-chiefs. Problems that involved women could also be handled by the queen mothers, who had their own linguists to help settle disputes. But the big cases went through the palace linguists—and many of them went through Kwame Boateng.

There were many rules involving appropriate dress and appropriate behaviour, and Okyeame Kwame Boateng knew them all. Akan traditional dress was made of wax-printed cloth or kente, worn with the right arm uncovered by the cloth. When greeting the king, one had to bend low and pull down the cloth on the left hand to show that nothing was hidden in the cloth, and also as a sign of respect. One had to learn how to put on the cloth so that it draped just right. Okyeame Kwame Boateng was perfect in that respect and people admired it.

Nonetheless, there were limits to his stature in the palace, of which he was only too aware. The stools used by Akan chiefs were made of purified carved wood (unlike most of the Guan kings who used animal skins). Libation was poured on the stools on certain specific days, invoking the dead ancestors of the kings of that particular stool. In the case of Okyeame Kwame Boateng, he had no black stool, as his position as okyeame was conferred on him; his stool was honorific, not ancestral. That meant that after his death, no member of his family could be appointed to succeed him to continue as palace linguist.

But Okyeame Kwame Boateng, who had taken on the position of linguist when he was a mere child, seemed to have made up his mind to be the best linguist in the Koforidua palace, even if his tenure lasted only for one lifetime. As it turned out, that tenure spanned several generations of kings, from Nana Asafo Boateng through Nana Kwaku Boateng II.

During that time, Okyeame Kwame Boateng saw much change in Ghana, but little in the chieftaincy. Akan kingship is a sacred office in Akan culture. Chiefs are accorded with respect and dignity—but like a pop star, they are often the victims of their own position. A chief or king could not be seen eating in public. Should he decide to eat when on a journey, he had to hide himself somewhere to chew in private. The king could not be seen in public unaccompanied. He could not cover his head with an umbrella by himself. His feet could not touch the ground in public, or that could lead to destoolment. And he must always be alert to the risk of spiritual attack from witches or wizards, and must fortify himself with potions to ward off curses. All these things Okyeame Kwamu Boateng observed and internalized, perpetually honing his skills in the service of his king.

13

Yaa Daben Starts a Family

Mr. Asianoa and Yaa Daben lived together happily and within three months of her wedding, Yaa was pregnant. Her husband was so thrilled that he started to buy the necessary things needed by an expectant mother, bit by bit, to make sure within the stipulated time of nine months, all the needed items would be ready. He made sure Yaa attended the local clinic regularly for checkups to ascertain the correct position of the baby and also the health of Yaa. And on a Sunday evening nine months later, Yaa Daben delivered a bouncing baby boy with black curly hair like his mother's.

Mr. Asianoa informed the family members of his wife's delivery, as Akan custom demanded. Gifts descended on Yaa as both family members and friends visited almost every hour of the day. On the seventh day, the naming ceremony was performed. The child was named Marfo after the father of Mr. Asianoa, and since he was born on Sunday, he was called Kwasi Marfo. The couple took great care of Kwasi Marfo, and Mr. Asianoa made sure his wife attended postpartum visits at the clinic at the end of every month, something most Akan mothers skipped due to illiteracy, ignorance, and the belief that herbal medicine was better than the white man's chemicals.

Marfo continued to thrive and within a year and a half had started walking. When Marfo was two years old, Yaa became pregnant again, and at the same time her younger sister Akua Badu became pregnant as well. They both delivered baby boys within two weeks of one another. Yaa delivered first on a Sunday and named the baby Kwasi Agyei, although he was generally called Gold Coast. Akua Badu delivered later on a Thursday and named her son Yaw Opoku, although he was later christened Fred Poku Sarkodee. The two grew together with their senior brother and cousin, Kwasi Marfo.

The Akan tribe believed in producing children and did not worry much about funds to care for them. They believed that their needs would be supplied through the grace of God through their ancestors. In view of that, Yaa was pregnant again in two years' time and delivered another baby boy, again on a Sunday. She named her third son Kwasi Akuoko (popularly known as Gambia).

During that time, a child could only be enrolled in school when the right hand could reach over the head and touch the left ear. They were not enrolled by age because most children did not know their ages, their parents being illiterate, and that was the only way to determine that their brains were developed enough to begin learning. However, at the age of five years, Marfo was enrolled in kindergarten at the Anglican school because of his father's influence.

At that time, the outfit used for school was a short-sleeved khaki shirt and khaki shorts to the knee—no sandals or shoes. Every morning, Mr. Asianoa could be seen holding the hand of his son Marfo, going to school in the same compound. He would walk his son to his class before entering his own classroom. It was delightful, and it encouraged some parents who, out of ignorance, had been reluctant to send their children to school, not knowing education was the key to success in life.

In ten years' time, Marfo completed the standard seven (middle school certificate). He taught briefly as an assistant teacher for eighteen months before enlisting in the Gold Coast Army in the West Africa Frontier Force, under the British colonial administration in 1943. He was stationed in Accra as a "home guard" during World War II to protect the colony from foreign attack. In 1944, at the age of 20, Marfo got married in Koforidua under the traditional marriage customs of the Akan people.

14

Birth of the Fulani Shrine

One Saturday afternoon in November 1945, a military jeep arrived in Koforidua from Accra (the headquarters of the military), which was about 80 kilometres away. It parked in front of the residence of Mr. Asianoa and his wife, and three military personnel got out of the vehicle. The military personnel addressed two young men in front of the house and asked to see Mr. Asianoa. The two young men introduced Mr. Asianoa to them. Mr. Asianoa gave them a seat and water as Akan custom demanded and asked them their mission. The sergeant broke the news that Marfo had developed a boil on his neck on Friday and had died the following day. They had been instructed by their superiors to inform the parents accordingly.

Mr. Asianoa broke down in tears like a baby. His wife, Yaa, screamed, threw her hands over her head, and wet herself. The sound of their grief attracted a lot of people into the house. Family members and sympathizers comforted them and when the storm had calm down in about half an hour's time, Mr. Asianoa requested that his son should be buried, not at the military cemetery in Accra, but at Koforidua, as they had a tradition to perform as they suspected foul play in Marfo's death. The sergeant obliged. The military, however, asked the family to inform them two days prior to the day of burial to enable them to bring the corpse from the military hospital and give him full military honours as a serving soldier.

Marfo's wife, who resided in her family house, was informed of her husband's death and she collapsed instantly. She was revived, however, by someone pouring water on her. She was five months pregnant. The family discussed the date of the burial and informed the military accordingly. On the day of the burial, the military brought the corpse in a coffin draped with a military flag and the pallbearers dressed in military uniform.

After everyone had filed past the coffin to give the deceased the last respect and farewell, Okyeame Kwame Boateng, the palace linguist and Marfo's uncle, had to pour libation. Okyeame Kwame Boateng was deeply touched by the death of his nephew. Strongly suspecting foul play, he had taken the lead in getting to the bottom of the matter.

Okyeame Kwame Boateng had his black cloth on, with his black native sandals, well polished to match. A bottle of schnapps and a glass were provided. He removed his cloth from the left hand downwards and removed his right foot from his sandal as a sign of respect for the gods and the ancestors. He raised his schnapps glass in the air to show to the Almighty his determination, and invoked the sacred mountain Obuo Tabri as he poured the drink on the ground, calling on his ancestors to avenge Marfo's death within forty days if it had not occurred naturally. He poured the drink to the ground like water, cursing whoever could have killed his nephew.

As he concluded the libation, tears flowed from the eyes of Okyeame Boateng. The Akan believed in life after death, and as such they normally presented a piece of cloth about one meter square that the dead could use to cover him or herself, and a small amount of money given to the deceased to buy water on the journey. Yaa, the mother of the deceased, tied one shilling six pence at one end corner of a black velvet cloth, folded it and place it in the coffin. The wife provided a white handkerchief and a ring.

Finally, the coffin was closed in order for it to be taken to the cemetery for burial. The coffin was carried by his peers, the military, tears rolling down the cheeks of almost everyone, grief being the price paid to the best and brightest who are lost too young. The wife of the deceased was prevented from going to the cemetery. Mr. Asianoa collapsed once more and was revived when the coffin was being lowered into the grave. Okyeame Kwame Boateng got drunk, fainted, and was also revived later. After the burial ceremony, sympathizers proceeded to the funeral grounds where they donated money to cover the funeral expenses, and grieving sentiments were exchanged amidst drumming, weeping, and traditional dancing as the norms of the Akan people decreed.

Exactly one month after the death and burial of Kwasi Marfo, there was another funeral in the town. The bereaved was a friend of Yaa Daben's. Yaa attended the funeral, which was for a child of about five and much less elaborate in scale than Marfo's. The elderly of the bereaved family met to pour libation early in the morning. Yaa, being a friend of the mother of the deceased, was asked to serve drinks in glasses to the elders.

As Yaa was going around with the tray of glasses filled with liquor, something unusual happened. It was as if a big stone hit the tray she was holding, and Yaa Daben suddenly fell on the ground with her two hands raised. She started murmuring some words, which could not be understood by anyone. She kept on repeating those words and the elders were astonished and did not know what to do. The elders approached her and one of them asked her in the Akan language, "Wose sen?" (What are you saying?) All they heard was "Fulani." (The Fulani are a primarily Muslim people scattered throughout many parts of West Africa from Lake Chad in the east to the Atlantic coast.)

Yaa repeated the word "Fulani" for a long time. The elders decided that whatever was affecting Yaa was a spiritual affair and they should call a Fulani man or woman to come and help them unravel the mystery. Two young men were asked to go to the outskirts of the town where there were a lot of Fulanis, to request their aid. Within a matter of about twenty minutes two Fulani men came and found Yaa still on the ground.

As soon as the two men approached, Yaa greeted them in the Fulani language, which is Fula. She asked them to listen carefully and inform the elders. She explained that a Fulani spirit had possessed her and the words coming from her mouth were not from Yaa but rather from the Fulani spirit. The spirit voice added that the young man, Kwasi Marfo, who died just about a month ago was killed by Yaa, his mother, through witchcraft and that Marfo had induced the Fulani spirit to possess her, not so her crime would be exposed and she would be executed, but so she would be persuaded to use her powers of witchcraft to help people who were in need.

The spirit continued that Yaa would wake up but would still be possessed by the male Fulani spirit. She would go home and start preparing her own shrine in her room in the family house (not in Mr. Asianoa's home) where she would do consultations, and from that day on she would be known as the Fulani priestess, or Komfo. Yaa had been completely initiated as a fetish priestess without the training normally required of fetish priests and priestesses. The spirit explained that his name was Abu, the head of the male spirits, but Yaa would sometimes be possessed by Magadjia, the head female spirit. When all of this was explained to the elders, they were dumbfounded.

Yaa rose up, still possessed by the spirit Abu, and accompanied by the two Fulani men and the elders, she went straight to the family house. Since the spirit that possessed her was a male one, she acted as a male. She entered her room and through the interpreters, the Fulani spirit requested that Yaa be supplied with clay, water, three cowrie shells, and an egg. From the clay mixed with water she built a shrine, in the form of a round hill about fifty centimetres in height and the same distance in diameter. She made a round hole at the top around which she placed the three cowries, and placed the egg in the hole.

The spirit then instructed that they should provide a smock, which Yaa would wear anytime the spirits possessed her, and further requested for traditional drums to enable the possessing spirits to dance. Abu, the male head spirit, thanked the Fulani interpreters, gave them some money, and wished them goodbye in the Fula language. At that moment Yaa became normal and asked the elders why there was white powder around her neck.

When all this was explained to her, Yaa bent her head and exclaimed, "My own son Marfo had exposed me!" She pleaded with the elders to inform Mr. Asianoa, and they agreed, proceeding to Mr. Asianoa's house.

Meanwhile, word had already reached Mr. Asianoa, but he did not understand it fully. When the elders entered, Mr. Asianoa gave them a seat and water according to Akan custom and requested to know their mission. The elders explained everything vividly to Mr. Asianoa. Mr. Asianoa asked them to help him pack his wife's belongings and send them to her, but they refused by saying that was not their mission. They asked for permission to depart, and left for their various homes.

Okyeame Boateng had travelled that day to a nearby village and returned from his trip around six o'clock. Upon hearing the rumors, he went to the home of one of the elders, who briefed him. He then went to see Mr. Asianoa, his brother-in-law, and after some discussions, Okyeame Boateng decided to help in sending all items belonging to Yaa to the family house. That was the end of the marriage. There was no family or church intervention.

Four months after the death of Marfo, his wife delivered a baby boy on a Saturday morning. The family of the deceased (Marfo) decided that the legal father of the newborn baby should be Yaw Poku (also known as Fred Poku Sarkodee), the nephew of Yaa Daben. It was agreed that the baby would not be told of any father other than Fred Poku Sarkodee. Fred Poku Sarkodee, who was then eighteen years old and a student, agreed to accept the responsibility of a father to avoid any explanation to the boy about how Marfo died. Moreover, it was decided that the baby would be given the name Kwame Poku—Fred Poku Sarkodee, Junior. Despite assuming responsibility for the child, Fred Poku Sarkodee Senior continued his education, proceeding to the Fora Bay College, Sierra Leone. From Fora Bay College, he continued to Britain to read law. Kwame Poku, in the meantime, grew to resemble his grandmother, Yaa Daben, and also his biological father, Marfo.

Okyeame Kwame Boateng, who lived in the same family house with his sister, never saw eye to eye with her. There was no peace between them. Whenever he was drunk, he would just pass in front of her room before going to his room without even greeting her. The Fulani priestess performed creditably, using local herbs to heal people of various ailments, and consulting about spiritual problems such as deflecting evil spells and overturning curses. She helped a lot of barren women get pregnant, most of who named their daughters after the Fulani female spirit (Magadjia).

The house was generally crowded with people who needed help, both physical and spiritual, from far and near. Food at the compound of the house was not a problem. Yaa always seemed to have plenty of money, and she could feed up to thirty people daily. Fufu and light soup was a daily affair every evening. But Kwame Boateng made sure his two grandchildren who were staying with him never ate his sister's food. He never trusted his sister, even as a Fulani priestess, as he believed she had killed his first daughter, Akosua Boatemaa. And why not? She had killed her own son.

15

The Secret Revealed

Fred Poku Sarkodee (Junior) began the Koforidua Anglican School in 1953 and completed the Standard Seven (Middle School Certificate) in 1962. At that time, he was staying in the family house with his grandmother, the fetish priestess, his biological father's younger brother Kwasi Akuoko (whom everyone called Gambia), and various other members of the family.

In the same year that Junior completed school, his adopted father, Fred Poku Sarkodee, Senior returned to Ghana from Britain as a qualified lawyer. When he took up appointment at the bench as a Magistrate in Accra, he took Junior with him and they stayed together as father and son. Junior was happy that the father had returned, and he looked forward to the opportunity of attending a secondary school like most of his peers. But he stayed with the father for over a year and half, and there was no sign that his education would continue, not even a discussion on it. He only did household chores, cleaned the house, washed the car, did the laundry—in short, he was being used as a houseboy.

The house where they lived had a main building and an outer house. The residence was walled with a gate guarded by a security officer. Junior lived in the outer house, while Senior lived with his wife and two children in the main building. One afternoon, while Senior was at work, his wife gone to her normal errands, and the children were at school, Junior heard a knock at his door. There was a man standing there dressed in a white shirt, black trousers, and black shoes. He was jet black in complexion with curly hair on his head.

The man greeted him in the Akan language by mentioning his name first—"Kwame, maaha" (Kwame, good afternoon). Junior responded in a confused manner because he did not know the man, though his face looked familiar and in fact, quite resembled Junior himself. Junior thought probably this was a family member he'd never met—not that surprising, since the Akan family is big. What was more puzzling was how the man could enter the main gate without the security officer informing him, and why he did not hear the sound of the gate opening as it normally did.

The man started by saying in the Akan language, "My name is Kwasi Marfo, and I am your real father, who died many years ago. Do not be afraid, as I have come to talk to you. The man you are staying with is my cousin, and he has no intention of helping you in any way. All I wish you to do is to go to your grandmother, Yaa Daben, the Fulani priestess, and tell her that she had colluded with my junior brother Gambia to claim the money the military was to pay to my beneficiary, which I had indicated on my enlistment form would be my child. They colluded and swore an affidavit that I had no child, even though at the time the money was paid out, you had been born."

Marfo then asked Junior to do all that it took to do the work of God, by preaching the gospel to mankind. He then gave him some money for transport back to Koforidua and finally, he gave him a small parcel containing a towel. He bade him goodbye and left. Junior wanted to see him off but the man declined.

When the man left, Junior immediately packed a few items and left for Koforidua without waiting for his adopted father to return from work. He left a message with the security officer at the gate that he was going to Koforidua. When he arrived in the evening at about four o'clock, he went to the family house occupied by his grandmother, the Fulani priestess. He asked her why she and his uncle had taken his inheritance. She requested to know who had informed him and he replied, "A man called Marfo came to me in broad daylight to introduce himself."

Yaa started screaming, "Marfo bioo!" (Marfo again, oo!). Junior immediately left and went to his mother's house to ask why after all those years, his own mother had not divulged that information to him. His mother explained that it had been a family consensus not to tell him. She asked, "But who did tell you?" Junior explained everything to her in detail and she sighed in relief. "Hmm, if not for your father, Kwasi Marfo, I never would have believed in the existence of ghosts."

She continued, "One month after you were born, which was about six months after his death, Marfo appeared to me in a dream and told me he was going to send some money to me to care for you." She went on to explain that the following day, she was at home when her sister rushed to her room to give her a parcel wrapped in a piece of cloth and covered with brown paper. Her sister informed her that the parcel was brought by a boy who mentioned another woman's name. The boy was asked to repeat the name of the other woman, but he replied, "Give it to your sister—she'll know whom it's from." When Marfo's wife opened the parcel, it contained two hundred pounds, which was good money at that time. And Marfo continued sending money to her through various means, sometimes appearing as an old man and sometimes as a boy. She concluded, "The money Marfo sent enabled me to start my food-stuffs business in the main market at Koforidua."

Junior's mother then told another very mysterious story about Marfo. Kwasi Akuoko (Gambia) had an affair with a woman trader who sold African hair dye. She used to hawk her wares in various towns, and one day she happened to be in the Tamale market in northern Ghana. As she was just about to close for the day, a young man approached her and asked her if she knew him and she said she did not. The young man told her the Fulani priestess was his mother, and he asked when she was going back to Koforidua. The woman said her wares were almost sold out and she had decided to go back in two days' time. The young man indicated that he would like to send a parcel to his mother and begged the trader to take it to her. The trader agreed, saying that Yaa was her mother-in-law (this trader had a baby girl with Gambia called Akosua Akyaa, named after the mother of Yaa Daben, whose name was Akyaa). The woman assumed the young man must be the offspring of one of the infertile women the Fulani priestess had helped.

The following day, almost at the same time, the young man returned with a parcel wrapped in brown paper. The woman collected it and he bade her goodbye. Upon reaching Koforidua, the woman sent the par-cel to the priestess. The Fulani priestess collected the parcel, opened it and to her astonishment, she found the parcel contained two tubers of yam and the black velvet cloth tied at one end of the cloth with one shilling and six pence, which was used in Marfo's burial.

That parcel sent a proverbial message in the Akan culture. If anyone intends to send a gift to someone dearly loved, three gifts should be sent, not two. Two tubers of yam meant the gift was not from the heart. The return of the black velvet cloth with money attached signified that Marfo did not need anything from his mother.

16

Suicide

In the early 1960s, the government of Ghana under the first president, Dr. Kwame Nkrumah, had introduced a compulsory free education for Ghanaian children and had established most secondary schools under the Ghana National Educational Trust Fund. That culminated in the establishment and expansion of boarding schools in the country's educational setup. To help boost the economy in the private sector and encourage Ghanaians to acquire entrepreneurial skills, private individuals were encouraged to serve as local food contractors to supply foodstuffs to schools.

Junior decided to enter into that venture and used some funds from his mother to commence business. Since his mother had been trading in foodstuffs for a long time, he started in Koforidua and later moved to Accra, the capital, to expand his business. He supplied foodstuffs such as plantains, yams, gari, beans, onions, and rice to secondary schools and teacher-training colleges both in Accra and Tema, a harbour city about 25 kilometres from Accra. The items were supplied to the schools on credit, after which payments were collected every three months in cash, upon submission of delivery of invoices to the school bursars.

With the trust established with his trading partners—the market women—he was able to access credit from them, paid quarterly when payments were made by the schools. Business was booming, so Junior decided to engage another person to assist him in his daily routine. He hired his Nigerian friend Rami, who had been his schoolmate in the Anglican school. They were able to add the University of Ghana to their list, and had to take more credit from the women traders to accomplish their task. Sometimes Junior had to go to Accra, while Rami went to Tema and vice versa. That continued for almost a year and a half. In the course of the business at the end of June 1966, Junior went off to Accra to collect his accumulated funds, and he sent Rami off to Tema to do the same, as the schools were going on a long vacation.

But Rami didn't come back with the money. It turned out that he had collected all the money from the secondary schools in Tema and taken off for Nigeria, never to be seen again. The funds Junior collected from the University of Ghana could not settle the debt he owed to the creditors, the market women who had trusted him. Shame was approaching and Junior could not face it.

He felt there was no solution, and determined to end it all. This gentle, sober-minded young man decided to commit suicide—an action that is a sin in the eyes of God and a crime before humanity. As Dr. Kwame Nkrumah said, "No one was born a criminal; it is the society that makes him so." Early one morning, he made sure that all the co-tenants in the compound house where he lived had gone to work and there was nobody home. He had prepared a potion of poison to end his life, and he didn't want to be rescued only to face more shame. He went to the main gate of the house to make sure no one was in sight, after which he planned to enter his room to commit the act.

Just as he was about to come inside, Junior heard someone calling him from behind, "Brother, brother, brother!" When he turned, he saw a small boy, about ten years old, running toward him with a brown bag. The boy approached him and said, "I am coming with your mother from Koforidua and she says to tell you that she's stopped to see someone on the way. Meanwhile, this is her bag and inside there's a wet towel. Your mother wants you to dry her towel for her and wait for her to arrive." Before Junior could say a word, the boy had run off.

Baffled, Junior wondered what his mother was doing in Accra. She had never visited him there and wouldn't know where he lived. He decided to dry the wet towel as he had been instructed, but lo and behold, there was no towel in the bag, only bundles of money. He sighed in relief and told himself, "If my mother has all this money, then why commit suicide? I will wait, and when she comes I will just ask her to help me pay off my debts to the creditors."

He waited the whole day and no mother came. As he slept that night, however, Marfo appeared to him in a dream. "Kwame, *I told you to go and spread the word of God.* I did not tell you to go into business. I have sent you this money to pay your creditors, and then I want you to do the work of God!"

When Junior woke up in the morning, he went to pay all the market women, packed his belongings and left for Koforidua. When he arrived, he went to tell his mother what had happened, and from there, he went to see the Anglican priest. He told the priest everything and expressed his desire to become a priest in the Anglican Church. The priest assisted him through the entire process, right up to his ordination. Fr. Fred Poku Sarkodee Junior has served in various Anglican churches in Ghana and is now in the United Kingdom, at St. Chad's Anglican Church in Hackney, London—still serving God at the age of 67.

Fr. Fred Poku Sarkodee preaching the word of God

Fr.Fred Poku Sarkodee leading other priests serving the Lord in St. Chad Anglican Church, Hackney London, United Kingdom

The Fulani priestess Yaa Daben died in 1979 after a short illness. After her burial, her son Kwasi Akuoko (Gambia) instructed his only male child, a boy of approximately sixteen at that time, to carry the Fulani shrine to his house near Adweso. As soon as the boy, Kudjoe, brought the shrine into the house, he instantly became insane. He is still parading the streets of Koforidua as a madman, thirty-two years after the death of the Fulani priestess. Gambia himself died about five years ago.

The lawyer/magistrate and adopted father of Junior, Fred Poku Sarkodee, rose through the ranks in the judicial service of Ghana to a high-court judge. He was one of the three high-court judges who, together with a retired army officer, were abducted from their homes and murdered in cold blood on the night of 30 June 1982. Their bodies were then doused with petrol and left in the bush at the Bundase shooting range. (The perpetrators of that wicked act attempted to burn the bodies, but were unsuccessful due to a heavy rainfall.) Okyeame Kwame Boateng once more poured libation for the family when he and the Justice's younger brother were asked to identify the body. He invoked the Obuo Tabri once more, praying that his ancestors might bring out the perpetrators of that heinous crime, and praying further that they should never know peace.

Two days after the pouring of the libation, the perpetrators were found. Three of the four murderers were tried and executed by a firing squad, but Sergeant Samuel Kwaku Amedeka, (the leader of the hit squad) escaped jail for Nigeria. He is now alleged to be living in Canada, still a fugitive.

Okyeame Boateng, a very good man, so fortified himself with juju (fetish) in his lifetime that it was difficult for him to die when it was time to join his ancestors. He was bedridden for a long time. In 1983, some fetish priests were called to remove some of the amulets/talismans hanging in his room so he could go to his maker.

Most of the younger generations in the family are strong Christians, considering what they had witnessed. Apart from the Anglican priest Fred Poku Sarkodee, other Christian leaders include Moses Omane Boateng (grandson of Okyeame Kwame Boateng and a pastor of the AME Zion Church, United States of America) and Elder Samuel Armah (Elder of the Pentecost Church, Ghana).

Many people in Africa have become victims of witchcraft attack and have sojourned to other countries, with no intention of ever returning to their place of birth. I wish to use this book to appeal to the witches and wizards in Africa, that they use their powers for the benefit of humanity, to build and not to destroy. It is not easy to fish in a river infested with reptiles and crocodiles (witches and wizards). In England, witches and wizards are openly showered with gifts during the festival of Halloween on the 31 of every October. Witches and wizards are not perceived as threats there because they don't engage in threatening behavior.

Nor are churches completely off the hook—far from it! Far too many pastors in Africa, particularly those presiding over nondenominational churches, use their pulpit to amass wealth at the expense of the members. This merely wards people away from churches and back into fetishism.

I wish to conclude this book by stating that no matter one's religious affiliation—be it Christianity, Buddhism, Islam, or Fetishism—no religious organization should be condemned, for God is the one who knows those that worship him. In addition, we should remember the words stated in the Holy Bible, in Ecclesiastes 12:13 which states, "Here is the conclusion of the matter: fear God and keep his commandments, for this is the duty of all mankind. For God will bring every deed into judgment, including every hidden thing, whether it is good or evil." All that must be known is that whether we believe it or not, everything in this world is spiritual, either positive or negative.

Finally, I pray that with the publication of this book the soul of Marfo will rest in perfect peace, and the spirit of insanity that has possessed Kudjoe for so many years will release him. It is my belief that the Fulani shrine, though it was born out of such deception and pain, did not come for the purpose of destruction but to be a focus for good in the world. May that be said of each one of us!

www.ingramcontent.com/pod-product-compliance
Lightning Source LLC
Chambersburg PA
CBHW030524290526
45786CB00004B/1607